# Table of Contents

# More than Beautiful

A Remarkable Story of Self-Love, Belonging and Kindness for today's woman

BRIGITTE ADOFO AGYAPONG

## Disclaimer

This is a parable with a motive to help readers use the lessons in this book to rule their lives, and not purely fictional.

Although this publication is designed to provide accurate information in regard to the subject matter covered, the publisher and the author assume no responsibility for errors, inaccuracies, omissions, or any other inconsistencies herein. This publication is meant as a source of valuable information for the reader. However, it is not meant as a replacement for direct expert assistance. If such level of assistance is required, the services of a competent professional should be sought.

## <u>Also Note that</u>

Names, characters, places, events and incidents, are all products of the author's imagination to tell the story and theme of this book. A resemblance to actual persons, living or dead, is purely coincidental.

For Bulk Purchase of this book, contact Brigitte on discounts@brigitteaagyapongwrites.com

# Note to you, my dear reader.

If I were to travel back to a time when I was a teenager and advise my younger self, this was what I would be telling her.

"Younger Brigitte, you have to be confident in yourself, love yourself and trust in your abilities.

What about yours? Is it similar to mine? If it is, have you done anything to help yourself overcome the self-doubt, denial and superpowers you have to possess to make life beautiful.

Most people battle with the ability to love themselves, and love the dark scars they dislike which they don't want the world to see. Are you the kind of person that people must praise before you see what you possess? There is a vast difference between knowing and not knowing your true self, but you are waiting for family and friends to tell you that you are beautiful, smart, intelligent, or any kind of trait before you give yourself the approval that you are what they say.

This is one of the reasons why "More Than Beautiful" is available to you now. The essence is to value yourself and your abilities, not people pleasing in order to be okay. I wanted to bring something that will create scenes and impact your minds and the wonderful hearts inside your chests.

I am glad to use the story of Lisa Mcshan to guide your ways. Fortunately for Lisa, she had some good people around her to turn her negative thoughts into positive ones and assist her in improving her personal development. People such as Lucy McCarthy, Davis Michaels and Coach Mike Gray were made available to guide her ways. I believe you are also ready to transform your life using this parable to change your mindset and values, and push towards self-love and gratitude. As you read this book, the key element I want you to grab is the lessons in it. Don't forget to share the message to help other loved ones improve their lives. Become an agent of transformation in other peoples' lives. Kindly share your review or opinion about this book on any marketplace you bought this book from, and this will help others to find their self-love and gratitude.

Enjoy your read.

Brigitte Adofo Agyapong

**Other books related to this book, More than Beautiful**

- *Gratitude Notes: An inspiring fable of gratitude and better living*
- *Lift it High: 58 motivational messages to uplift your dreams into reality for maximum success and elevation.*
- *Better than Half. An inspiring story to find peace in the midst of dismay*

**Journals**

- Emotional mastery journal
- Emotional Release Journal
- Mood Tracking Journal

# Dedication

To every woman around the world who wants to love the darkest scar in their lives, I want to use this book to tell you yes, you can love yourself too.

# Acknowledgement

To everyone who has helped share the message of hope, possibilities, and greatness in any way, thank you.

# Introduction

Do you feel the need to fit in to be okay with people? Are you waiting for people to acknowledge you before you perform? What causes you to experience that? More Than Beautiful is a remarkable story of self-love, belonging and thankfulness. It will tackle your experience with the help of storytelling. Lisa's story will shape our thoughts and feelings to own and love ourselves and, on top of that, practice the habit of kindness.

It is a parable of clearing all the pain from our bodies and believing in our abilities.

Lisa McShan is a successful young lady who is steering the furniture industry. She is the Ceo of Lisa Initiatives LLC. She is an inspiration to other women because of what she has achieved. Aside from other women, people in the community look up to her to grow their companies, just like she did. Due to effort, she is known as the successful Lisa.

She has a goal. The goal is to win a 100 million tender contract to deliver furniture to Event and Associates, a top brand in West Avenue and beyond. Her eyes and body are so fixed on this goal. She imagines that she could open more branches when this happens, become more popular and, above all, impress her loving mother and, most importantly, the people who once looked down on her.

Due to the desire and energy on this goal, even when other opportunities come her way, she never sees them as opportunities. All her focus is on the 100 million contract.

The effect draws her into a journey that makes her revisit the pain and experiences of her past, both from childhood and adulthood.

Wondering what will happen to Lisa, the result of the tender and her journey to self-discovery, self-love and happiness?

Get ready, and ride with Lisa to find her authentic self and live a happier life.

# The Contract

She settled down at the back of her car holding the document and wondered why things had to go wrong this time. Lisa believed that, this time, her company would win the prestigious contract.

Less than 48 hours ago, she was excited for this and couldn't imagine the sudden end.

Her hopes had been crashed, leading her to fume for the incident with a rapid heartbeat.

"I knew no one liked me. I am not loved. Why was I expecting to win? You are a failure, Lisa!." She mutters to herself.

With a frown on her face and a lot of thoughts running through her brain, she repeated those negative words to herself.

Her mind took her back to a few minutes ago in the office of Mr. Micheals.

She gazed and smiled to herself, as she placed her left feet on the parking lot of the 5 storey glass building, lifting herself from the back seat of her orange 4-wheel drive. Lisa pushed the door closed as she straightened her black ladies suit.

Her face rounded and looks amazed at what she believed would happen to her in that office. The joy of winning tagged at her heart.

"Daniel, kindly park the car at the far end" she instructed.

"Please, this is where the car must be parked; at the right side a few spaces away from the exit. Don't move until I return from the meeting," She revealed. Daniel nodded, as she gave way for Daniel to position the car to the directed space.

She looked up at the tall building of Events and Associates, and had no doubt in her mind that she was going to be the right candidate to win the contract this time around. Events and Associates was fond of organizing remarkable events in the area of West Avenue and beyond, which included both corporate and social events. She had a sure expression on her face, which made her believe she was going to take the title.

She murmured, "Am I the one who is about to win this contract? I can't believe that I was invited by Davis himself to meet him for the contract." Her face continued to round up and her cheeks slowly shifted upwards.

She walked gracefully to the entrance as the security man at the gate ushered her in. "Welcome ma'am," he greeted. She nodded, and smiled in affirmation.

She padded through to the front desk. As soon as she was an inch to the reception table, the receptionist stood up and greeted with a smile, "Welcome, madam Lisa. Let me make a call to Mr. Davis to inform him that you are in."

Lisa, with a smily face, though she was still surprised on the kind of gesture she had just received, replied "Why not? That is why I am here".

After the phone conversation, the receptionist announced, "You may go in," as she pointed to the entrance of the fourth floor. "Kindly use the elevator. It's the second office on the left." she continued.

"Okay, I got it." Lisa acknowledged.

Lisa followed the directions of the receptionist, and on the 4th floor, on the left, she knocked on the door with the inscription CEO, Mr. Davis Michaels.

"Come in please," she heard, and gently opened the door into his office. Upon seeing her, Mr Michaels hailed her with all the accolades he knew about her. "Lisa McShan, I have heard a lot of great things about your firm. I'm glad to have you in my wonderful office. Please have a seat." He directed her to sit.

"Would you care for water?" he asked.

"That's ok," she replied.

As she moved, she was a bit surprised but filled with hope. Lisa sat on a soft black chair, which was opposite her host.

"Thank You, Davis, it is a great privilege to be in your office." she said as she made herself comfortable.

"I am so glad you honoured my invitation. How is business? And how is your distribution going? He asked politely.

"Business is going well, and we're looking to expand our reach to additional areas across the country. Our goal is to increase distribution, particularly to companies that organize events. We aim to supply these companies with items like concert chairs and other event accessories." she responded.

"Although Lisa Initiatives LLC initially focused on distributing corporate furniture and fixtures, that line has become somewhat seasonal. To stay active and promote growth, we've expanded our product offerings rather than waiting for sales to pick up. We're constantly learning and adapting every day to keep the company moving forward." She explained further.

"You are right, we also want to add up to the concert and festivals to bring spice to the product lines, too, since our brand is well known for organizing and managing corporate conferences and other social events like weddings, parties, birthday parties". He responded.

"We decided to bring spice to attract attention in those areas since we have been successful in the minds of users for the organizing and management of events for over 20 years now."

"Yea, I believed so, and it is good to explore other areas in our business chains whilst we have the opportunities as business personnel," she replied, opening to his conversations.

"Lisa, do you know something?" He asks, to which Lisa responded, "No."

"Do you know the qualities I like about your business and you as their leader?"

She yearned to find more. With ears attentive to hear more, she responded with a shy smile, "Tell me. I would love to hear it. Let it flow."

"Okay, I will." He said and continued.

"Areas I wish my business would learn from your business is the customer service and quality products you have on board. Though my business has not done much with you, I have personally used your rectangle wooden desk for four years and it's still in good shape. I have friends who are into businesses just like me who patronized your products. I really like the extent of the durability of your materials and customer service."

"Since we are humans with imperfect experiences, we cannot be perfect in all areas. It is great to learn from the best as they also learn from you." He said.

"May I know some of your friends who have use my products, I would love to know?" She quizzed. "Alpha group," he responded.

With a tap on her forehead, she cheerfully continued, "Oh, yea, Alpha group is one of my loyal customers and I am not surprised they recommended me. It's been 5 years doing business with them, and they keep recommending me. In fact, I love what they do".

"Absolutely. That is great," Davis continues.

"I have heard news about your customer services, and I would love to learn from you." He confided.

She mused, "My work was not appreciated by my customers because I only receive bad reviews, so I believe I am not loved".

"Did you say my product has been in use for four years now?" She enquired.

"Oh yes, four years and it's still in good shape." He responded

She still wondered why it was possible. She smiled, "Yes, quality comes first, followed by our customer service. I believe our customers—just like you—are one of the biggest factors in our company's growth. We want to care for them sincerely, to empathize with their needs. Their concerns should be our concerns, and we must provide products that truly help them. Above all, the durability of our materials is essential." Lisa spoke.

"Every word you said here is true for customer service and quality. That is why I think I can learn something from you," Davis complimented.

"Thank you for the compliment, Davis." She beamed with a broad smile.

He took a document from his cabinet and positioned it at the centre of the table.

"When I saw your application submission for our furniture tender request, I was glad to see that you had applied. That is one of the reasons why I called to have you in my office to personally inform you about the result and whether or not you have won the contract."

Her smile dropped a little, as he informed her.

"You have to keep in mind that whatever be the results I, Davis, sill wants to do business with you."

"Exactly, that is the main reason why I came here, per the email you sent." Lisa clarifies.

"I realized that you missed two document, which was supposed to be attached to the proposal during the in-person delivery at this premise. Though, I am the Chief Executive Officer here, I could not do anything. The procurement department makes the final decision, and they are governing by rules and policies. Rules are rules, you know?"

She nodded with the faintest smile.

"I don't have that power; I couldn't change it. This is the result; it is that you didn't win the 100 million contract."

Upon hearing the news, she kept quiet for a minute to catch her breath before she could speak again

"Why, did you reject my application? I made sure that everything was on point." She lamented.

"Lisa, everything was on point, but you know this contract was worth 100 million in value and we needed to make sure you had good financial standing to partially pre-finance the project. None of the evidence document was attached, and clientele stories were also not attached. That is the main standpoint you need to win this kind of tender. We wanted to see the financials to convince us. Your firm brought none." He explained.

Lisa kept quiet as he gave more update.

"I know you are a successful businesswoman who will not compromise on opportunities when they come. Unfortunately, this time, it did not come your way. That is why before I announced the results, I gave you a caveat that whatever happens, we are ready to do business with you. We have multiple collaborations and partnership each time. I believe there are reasons why things happen in life. More opportunities will come. Just trust the process. Don't worry for now. You just must be ready to deliver when it comes. Now, this is the new avenue for you. We want to partner with you to distribute corporate chairs to 45 clients on our database. But before we finalized, I will invite you in again to discuss more partnership and contract opportunities." He concluded.

"Why do you still want to give me another contract after losing this one? Do you think my firm is worthy to deliver?" She asked curiously.

"Hmm, Lisa, you see, your firm is one of the top furniture distributors here in the West Avenue area and beyond. You're the best, with top-notch service, and I'd be making a big mistake if I didn't award you this contract. But for the 100-million project, my hands are tied—I can't do anything about it. If you're worried that a competitor has overtaken you, don't be. No one in this country won that contract; it was awarded to an international company," he replied, reassuring Lisa.

"Yes, when one opportunity closes, another opens—same company. I'm glad to be working with you on this project and look forward to finalizing everything soon. It's a pleasure to meet you in person, Mr. Michaels, and I'm excited to build a strong partnership with you."

After she accepted the results of the tender, Davis handed her a letter enclosed in an envelope. Lisa smiled as she received it.

"I think the main reason for this meeting is clear. Is everything clear, Lisa?" Davis urges.

"Absolutely. I think everything is clear. We will be waiting for your invitation again to talk more about the other contract."

They both exchanged business cards.

"Okay, I will take my leave, and I will communicate with you via phone or email," Lisa assured.

Davis stood from his soft black chair and Lisa also rose from her seat. They both shared a handshake and a hug.

As she walked out and closed the door behind her, she wondered why she'd been awarded the small contract instead of the bigger one. "There was a major contract I could have landed. We have the capacity to deliver—why didn't he choose us?" she thought. She headed straight to the elevator, pressed the button to the ground floor, and soon appeared at the front desk.

She gave a wave and smiled at the receptionist.

At the entrance, her soft expression change to a furious one as she walked to her orange car and sat in it.

During that reflection, she crumbled the cover letter she had received from the Mr. Michaels in her left hand.

"Move the car," she commanded. "I said, move the car, driver," She shouted again, and with a stern expression from the driver, he moved.

# Still ponders.

"Ma'am, we're here," Daniel called out as he parked the car. She raised her left hand to her stomach and glanced at her wristwatch. "You took 30 minutes to drive here from 7th Avenue to 5th Street. It's usually only 15 minutes to the office."

"There was a traffic jam on the road, Madam Lisa," he replied.

"Alright, never mind. You can park in the underground lot," she said, stepping out of the car. She looked up at the four-story office building, her gaze settling on the showroom that occupied the ground and first floors. "All this space, all these assets filled with furniture, and they say I don't have the capacity to deliver," she thought, shaking her head in disbelief. She slowly walked to her office on the second floor.

Once inside, she instructed her secretary, Joyce Mintah, "Don't allow anyone into my office unless I tell you to, okay?" Joyce nodded, agreeing to follow her instructions. Lisa closed the door firmly behind her, exhaled a tired sigh, and took a chilled bottle of water from the mini fridge near the door.

She sank into the green, plush sofa. "Today has been so stressful, even though it shouldn't have been," she murmured. Her eyes drifted to some documents on her wooden desk, and her mind wandered back to Davis's office and the disappointment of his announcement. She vividly remembered the experience, the emotions that surged through her when he said she hadn't won the 100-million project. The intense anticipation she'd carried into that meeting was undeniable.

Her stomach churned as her heartbeat quickened, the usual signs of tension and frustration welling up inside her. "I wish I could have shouted so loud that the whole world would hear me when he said, 'You didn't win it,'" she thought, her face tightening in frustration.

After a moment, she stood up, refocused, and moved to her black office chair at the rectangular wooden desk. She opened her i10 Core laptop, which was still on her email page from earlier that morning, and scrolled through her inbox with a busy look, searching for the email that had led to today's meeting.

"Oh, yea here it is," she whispered and clicked on it.

She read.

*Dear Lisa Mcshan,*

*I trust you are good.*

*This is Davis Michaels, The CEO of Events and Associates. I would love to have a meeting with you to discuss the announcement of the result of the tender of the concert chairs distribution contract and other business collaboration with you.*

*Kindly let me know your acknowledgement on this.*

*Looking forward to your prompt reply.*

*Kind Regards*

*Davis Michaels*

*CEO, Event & Associates*

As she read, her thought took her back to the experience she encountered when she received it for the first time on 12<sup>th</sup> January. She was cheerful and could not wait to read it and meet him in person.

She read her reply to his email.

*Dear Mr. Michaels,*

*Thank you for reaching out to us here at Lisa Initiatives LLC.*

*On behalf of this firm, I appreciate the effort to invite me personally to your office to discuss the result of the tender.*

*Is 15<sup>th</sup> January, 9am GMT okay for you?*

*Kindly let me know your confirmation.*

*Looking forward to your response.*

*Kind Regards,*

*Lisa McShan,*

*CEO*

*Lisa Initiatives LLC*

She read and gave a beautiful stare as she continued to read the email thread.

*Dear Miss McShan,*

*The scheduled date and time is perfect for me. Can you schedule the meeting with my receptionist, Brand Michaels, on 092 4858 942 to book your place.*

*I can't wait to meet you.*

*Looking forward to a fruitful meeting with you.*

She smiled briefly, but her face stiffened as she reflected on the excitement she once felt, only to be humbled by the reality. Lost in thought, she picked up her phone and called Joyce. "Don't make any mistakes. Call this number, 092 4858 942, and schedule a meeting with Mr. Davis Michaels and me. Let me know once it's confirmed," she instructed.

Her expression darkened, her lips pursed tightly as the memories flashed by, barely containing her frustration. She replayed the events in her mind, questioning if all the required documents were correctly submitted with the application and wondering who might be responsible if they weren't. She hadn't personally assembled the paperwork for the tender.

With a loud snap, she closed her laptop forcefully and reached for the office phone to call Joyce again—the second call that day. She needed answers.

"Joyce, call in the development team responsible for the concert chair proposal to my office. Now!" she commanded, hanging up the phone with a thud.

# I blame you

A knock sounded at the door.

"Come in," Lisa responded.

The development team entered her office in sequence. Evans Watson stepped in first, followed by Evana Attah and Steven Josephs. Each wore a tense expression, as if they already sensed the gravity of the situation.

Lisa folded her arms across her chest as they approached, her face set in a hard line, clearly preparing to let loose. Evans moved forward and began to pull a visitor's chair out to sit.

“Who told you to sit down? Your colleagues are still standing there. Do you think you're more important than them?” Lisa shouted, her voice sharp. Evans looked startled, shaking his head in submission.

"No, madam," he replied, quickly moving back to stand with his teammates, who watched with wide eyes, visibly taken aback by the exchange.

Lisa sighed. "I know you're surprised by my reaction, but I'm not satisfied with the work you did. Something went wrong with the concert chair distribution proposal."

Steven looked confused. "Ma'am, we don't know what's going on. Based on how we've been received here, unless you tell us, we have no idea what happened."

"Who among you prepared the proposal?" Lisa asked, her eyes blazing.

"We all worked on it," they replied in unison, gesturing to show they had collaborated.

"Who gathered the documents?" she pressed.

Steven raised his hand slightly. "I did."

"And who made sure all the necessary documents were attached?"

With a firm voice, Evana responded, "I did, madam."

"Lastly, who reviewed the proposal to make sure we understood it fully?"

"I did," Evans answered.

"Evans, you're the team leader. Your role was to read through the procurement documents, understand them thoroughly, and ensure your team did too. I'm talking about the concert chair proposal."

"Yes, madam—the Events & Associates tender," he replied. "We knew it mattered to you, so we took our time to get it right."

"You *took your time*! Are you telling me that?" Lisa's voice rose. "Absolutely not—you did the opposite."

Turning to Evana, she continued, "And you, Evana, your responsibility was to check every requirement and document, especially to catch any errors Evans might have missed."

"Oh, madam, I ensured everything was in order," Evana responded defensively.

"Be quiet, Evana. You did the opposite here," Lisa snapped. Evana fell silent under Lisa's glare.

"Team," Lisa continued, tapping her fingers on the table, "do you realize that we missed two essential documents that should have been attached? We lost that contract because of this."

At that moment, the office door opened, and Lucy McCarthy entered. Lisa's expression darkened as she addressed her, "And you—what are you doing here?"

Ignoring the warning in Lisa's voice, Lucy walked in, maneuvered past the team to the green sofa, crossed her legs, and folded her arms, appearing unfazed by the tension in the room. Lisa sighed, the team looking back and forth between her and Lucy in shock.

Lisa redirected her attention to the team. "We missed two documents that were critical for this bid—financials and the client testimonials. Because of that, we lost the 100-million contract to another company. How could you let this happen?" She pointed at each of them as she spoke. "I am so disappointed in all of you."

Steven hesitated, then asked, "Ma'am, what were those missing documents?"

Lisa's face flushed with frustration. "Are you asking me? You were careless! I needed this contract, and you overlooked it. How dare you?"

"We're sorry," they replied together.

"The missing documents were our financials and client testimonials. That's right, you missed them," Lisa said sternly.

"Yes, madam, we missed it, and we're sorry about that," Evana replied softly.

"Well, being sorry isn't going to change what's done. I've made up my mind on this," Lisa said firmly. "As a consequence, I'm reducing all of your monthly salaries by 15%."

Their eyes widened in disbelief at her decision.

Evana pleaded, "Please, it won't happen again."

Lucy intervened, "Lisa, why are you doing this to such a wonderful team? Please, don't be so hard on them."

"Shut up, Lucy. Don't interfere in my business." Lisa snapped, and Lucy leaned back on the sofa, withdrawing.

Lisa turned back to her team. "Listen to me—until I see real change in our work, this punishment stands. I trusted you all. I believed I had a strong team behind me to elevate this company, and you gave me the opposite."

"How could you let this happen?"

"But, ma'am..." Evans began.

"No buts. I'm done here. Go back to your work," Lisa said firmly.

The team looked down, defeated, and filed out of the room one by one. As they left, Lisa cast a regretful glance at Lucy, her friend's presence stirring a mix of anger and disappointment within her.

She opened her mouth slightly, as if about to say something to Lucy, but the words seemed heavy, refusing to leave her lips. Instead, she tapped her index finger on the desk, her gaze shifting between the table and her friend.

Lucy, feeling the weight of Lisa's stare, looked back at her friend briefly before averting her eyes to a distant corner of the room, equally reluctant to voice what was on her mind.

# Recommendation by a friend.

Lisa cleared her throat. "S-sorry... Sorry, Lucy," she stammered, visibly agitated. She stood, retrieved a juice from her fridge, and walked over to Lucy. "I'm sorry for what I did."

"Sorry for what?" Lucy asked gently.

"You know, for shouting at you in front of my team," Lisa admitted, her tone remorseful. "I was furious about what they did. The impact of their mistakes is still boiling inside me, and I just can't accept it." She handed Lucy a glass of coconut-pineapple juice. "Here, your favorite drink—coco-pine juice."

"Thank you," Lucy replied, smiling as she took a sip. "Do you know why I accepted this? It means I've forgiven you."

"I couldn't believe you shouted at me with such anger and then lashed out at your staff like that," Lucy continued. "The Lisa I know wouldn't raise her voice, even when things go wrong. It was like seeing a different person just now."

"If you really were the person I saw a few minutes ago, I would have walked out of this office. But I know that's not you, Lisa. There's something weighing on you, something big. So... can you tell me what's wrong?"

"Thank you for accepting my apology," Lisa said softly, lowering her gaze. "You're right... I don't know why I acted that way, but I feel so weighed down by everything. I wish shouting could fix it; I can't seem to calm down."

"I knew it," Lucy said. "I could tell something was off. We've known each other for 15 years. If you open up to me, maybe I can help or at least offer some advice. C'mon, tell me."

Lisa hesitated, unsure whether to reveal what was truly troubling her. But she knew Lucy wouldn't let it go until she found out. Finally, she took a deep breath.

"I guess you overheard me asking them about that contract," Lisa began.

"Yes, I did," Lucy replied, nodding encouragingly.

"Okay," Lisa began, her voice heavy with frustration. "Lisa Initiatives LLC applied for a tender with Events & Associates to distribute concert chairs for their events. We lost because two major documents—the financials and testimonials—were neglected by my team. We didn't win."

"I think more opportunities will come. You have to cool down," Lucy encouraged gently.

"What? Cool down? Oh no, do you know the worth of that contract and what the firm could have gained from it? Please don't tell me that—you'll just raise my temper again!"

"Okay, still, you have to cool down," Lucy insisted.

"I'm not going to do that! This contract is worth 100 million! This is huge!"

"Whether it's 1 million or 100 million, you must calm down. Just because you've lost one opportunity doesn't mean you've lost others. More will come."

Lisa chuckled, a bitter edge to her laugh. "You don't know what I could do with that money. The profit would allow us to expand to other locations, people would finally know us. I mean, we'd be popular, and most importantly, my mother would appreciate me more. All those who've looked down on me would finally respect me."

Lucy tapped her palm against her forehead, exasperated. "I've told you this countless times: you can't focus on the opinions of others to feel okay. You can't impress everyone. All this yelling at your team is just about trying to impress people. From what I know about your firm, the activities you do here are worth more than 80 million. I believe this shouldn't be a big deal."

"Lisa, face reality and stop dreaming. I've told you many times to focus on yourself. Even with all the good things you do, your mother doesn't appreciate your efforts. She never acknowledges you as a good daughter bringing honor to her. Please, I urge you to love yourself and be yourself."

Lisa's voice softened. "I care about my mother's acceptance; it's a big deal for me. It's one of the reasons I was so furious with my staff."

"Please don't do this to yourself. Someone needs to help redefine your mindset because your thoughts are corrupted by the idea of your mother's acceptance."

"Do you believe in yourself?" Lucy asked.

"Yes, I do. Why do you ask?" Lisa responded defensively.

"Your actions say otherwise. You don't appreciate what you have; you feel you have to impress people to be loved. I sincerely think you need a change in your life, especially if you're putting the blame for your personal desires on your staff. Please, you need to change."

"I didn't like punishing them, but I had to do it," Lisa replied, her voice tinged with regret.

"I agree with your statement about not believing in what you possess. Can you imagine that Davis told me he likes my business and what I do?"

"And do you believe what he said?" Lucy inquired, raising an eyebrow.

"I doubted it at first. The customer reviews I get are mostly bad. I didn't believe him, but I played along. It still amazes me what he said."

"Are you telling me you haven't received any good reviews from customers?" Lucy asked, a hint of disbelief in her tone.

"I have a lot of them; it's just that the bad testimonials drain me. I wish I could have zero bad reviews," Lisa responded, her frustration evident.

"Then why are you focusing on the bad reviews instead of believing in yourself?" Lucy probed.

"I feel like 100% of my customers should like my products and what I do. I've tried to change that thought, but I can't seem to shake it," Lisa admitted.

"I need you to relax and be calm. Don't bring your worries to your team. It's not their fault; they'll learn from their mistakes. I'm not an expert, but the only thing I can recommend is this." Lucy handed her a business card.

Lisa took the card and looked at it. "A coach? What do I need a coach for? I'm already doing well; I'm a founder of a business, so I don't need it."

"I'm glad for once you're acknowledging your quality as a successful businesswoman, but you will need a coach to guide you and help redefine your mindset—or even learn to love yourself. A life coach isn't just for the weak; it's for everyone. Just give it a try."

"I remember I've received this card from you five times now," Lisa confirmed, flipping the card over in her hand.

"See, this is a test. The most important thing is that you have a willingness to change inside of you. Give yourself the chance," her friend advised.

"I will," Lisa responded, a hint of determination creeping into her voice. "Oh, it's like he's very close by. Thank you, Lucy."

# An encounter with Coach

"Let me call before I forget," Lisa assured her friend. She took out her phone to make the call.

"Hello, am I speaking to Coach Michael Gray?" Lisa began the conversation.

"Yes, you are. Oh wait, this voice sounds familiar... Oh! Lisa McShan on my line! Finally, you called!" Michael Gray responded, his enthusiasm evident.

"How did you get my name?" she demanded, a hint of curiosity in her tone.

"Oh, your name? Everyone in this area knows you. Lisa, the successful woman! Your friend assured me you would be calling for a discovery call, but I've been waiting for you for years. It seems today is a special day for me," Michael replied.

"Coach, it sounds like you're flattering me," she complimented, feeling a bit bashful.

"Did you say I'm successful?" Lisa questioned, wanting to gauge his sincerity.

"Oh yes, you are! You're doing great things for yourself and your business. Everyone in this area and beyond knows you as one of the successful women in this country. I've heard great testimonials about you; you've become a pacesetter for other women in entrepreneurship and business. You're an inspiration to others," Michael answered.

"Well, that's what others say. Sincerely, I don't believe I'm successful. If I were, I would have won one of the big-time opportunities in my life. I feel like I'm just working, not truly successful," Lisa replied, her voice tinged with doubt.

"Why do you say that, Miss McShan?" he asked, intrigued.

"From my childhood experiences and other events in my adult life, I've learned that I can't be successful. What people see as success, I see as just hard work. I feel like an empty container that can't hold anything good inside," she confessed, her vulnerability surfacing.

With a cheerful voice, Michael responded, "Wow, that's quite powerful. How can I help you?"

With a soft voice and a naïve expression, she continued, "From my friend Lucy's awareness, I realized I need change in a lot of areas in my life. Though I'm seen as successful in business, I feel like there's nothing good going on inside me. I'm not happy in my personal life."

With a curious tone, he probed further, "Why do you feel you're an empty container?"

"I feel a sense of not belonging. I don't trust my abilities and often want to impress people. I'm obsessed with it, like I'm heavily burdened by that need. When no one praises me, I feel like I'm nothing—unhappy and alone. I want to be treasured by the people I love, but I'm not receiving much. I feel like a failure," Lisa confessed, her voice trembling slightly.

"Noted on this, Lisa. I will do my best to help and guide you on whatever mission you have inside of you, especially concerning your personal life," Coach Michael assured her.

Lisa clenched her fist and tapped on the table in front of her. "The reason I'm telling you this, coach, is that I don't often open up, even to Lucy. She hasn't heard any of this from me."

He replied calmly, "I feel your instinct is telling you something—maybe it's time to give way for change, Lisa. I think you trust her this time."

"Are you ready to be coached?" he asked gently.

"Coach, it feels like you're in my body! I have this strong energy for change to happen. I want to free myself and be happy," Lisa exclaimed, her enthusiasm growing.

"You will if you're ready to be coached or guided," he assured her.

"I'm strongly ready for this since I want to throw away over 20 years of worries and my desperate need to be loved."

"I've been wondering about this: why do you and your friends all have the same initials, L.M.?" he inquired curiously.

"Oh, no!" she smiled, realizing it for the first time. "I hadn't considered that at all. Maybe destiny brought us together for her to be an avenue to transform my inner child."

"Yeah, I believe so. When would you like to have your first appointment with me? By the way, you can call me Coach Mike," he continued.

"Well, according to my calendar, January 17th at 10 a.m. works for me," Lisa replied.

"Okay, accepted! The date is perfect for me too. See you on the 17th at 10 a.m.," he confirmed.

Lisa hung up the phone with a beaming smile. "Wow, Lisa, I'm so happy for you! You're willing to change for the better. Please ensure you communicate with him if you can make it to your sessions. Good luck with your session with him!" Lucy praised her with a cheerful countenance.

"Thank you, my dear! Speaking to him felt like clearing a pinch of my worries away. It's like I already know him. The energy and connection are strong. He didn't judge me like you did. I feel comfort with this coach, even though this is my first time. I have a positive feeling inside that something big is coming my way. Thank you so much!"

She stood and spread her arms to hug Lucy tightly.

"Wait, Lisa!" Lucy called out as she was about to give her a warm hug. "So now I'm judging you? You know I'm not a coach, so that encounter will surely be different."

"I'm so sorry if those words gave a different meaning!" Lisa assured, a hint of concern in her voice.

Lucy chuckled, "I'm joking!" She hurriedly embraced her friend in a playful, dancing way. "I can't wait to see you transform into the new Lisa McShan! I'm ready to assist you, maybe as your accountability partner to help you along the way."

"I'm ready, my dear accountability partner!" Lisa responded enthusiastically.

"See you later!" Lucy advised as she moved out of Lisa's office. " And please, don't open any emails or do anything that will trigger the experiences from today."

"Don't worry, I will take that advice!" Lisa replied with a joyful grin. "See you later!"

As Lucy left, Lisa felt a renewed sense of hope and excitement for the changes ahead. She knew that with the support of her friend and the guidance of Coach Mike, she was on the path to finding her true self and happiness.

# Getting ready for self-improvement

Her face was filled with a nervous look as she pulled her chair a little forward, waiting for the coach. Lisa felt like this was her first time stepping out of her office or home for an appointment aimed at personal transformation. It was a new experience, and her body trembled with a mix of fear and excitement about the changes ahead.

As Coach Mike entered his office, he greeted her warmly and settled into his chair, ready to begin their session. "Oh no, Lisa, what's up? Your face doesn't look very light today."

She babbled a bit before answering, "Um, I'm excited to be here, but I'm kind of shaken inside. I know a lot of stuff needs to come out of me today."

"Everything will be okay," Mike reassured her. "Think of me as your trusted friend. Let's take a deep breath in and out. Let's try it and see what happens."

Lisa followed his instructions, inhaling deeply and then exhaling slowly.

"Are you okay now?" he asked, observing her closely.

"Better than before," she admitted. "Sitting here in this hot seat with you—it's like your presence has eased me a little."

"I'm glad to hear that," he said. "But I believe you might experience a mix of emotions after our encounter today."

She sighed, a sign of relief.

He brought his palms together, resting them on the table, his elbows at the edges. "Lisa, welcome to my wonderful abode. How may I help you?"

Lisa looked surprised by his warm welcome. She murmured to herself, "I thought we spoke on the phone two days ago, and I shared what was worrying me. With this question, I don't get it." Nevertheless, she responded, "Well, I'm here because..."

Before she could elaborate, Mike interrupted gently. "Lisa, don't be surprised. I know we spoke, but I need to hear more about what you're experiencing to understand why you're sitting in front of me today. Can you tell me what brings you here, to my coaching corner, if I may say?"

Lisa smiled and responded affirmatively, "Two days ago, we had a call to see what's up with me. I feel empty inside. Even though I've received countless praises for what I do, I don't see myself that way. In my head, I feel like a failure just working and not the successful person the world sees me as. I'm empty within.

I want to change a lot of things. I think I need to bring up my tendency to be a people pleaser, especially for my mom. I believe everything has to be perfect, and I have all these different views about myself and the people around me. I need change."

Mike listened intently, gazing at her with keen interest. "You said it right. But in order to help you succeed, you also have to be ready to change and apply every tool I introduce here. Take it one step at a time."

Lisa agreed with the coach's instructions, her anticipation for new beginnings evident in her joyful smile.

"You've mentioned many things about yourself and what you want to change. Why do you believe you're a failure, even though you've achieved a lot and the world knows you as successful Lisa?"

"I don't actually know," she replied. "I know nothing in this world is okay. It feels off; I don't feel competent with what I have. Each time I want more."

Michael nodded thoughtfully. "And does this make you happy when you measure yourself like this?"

"It's like you're driving me to something," she admitted. "From the outside, people see me as a happy person, smiling all the time, but inwardly, I'm not happy because I think I'm not successful. I have to impress key people in my life, like my beloved mother. She is everything to me. If she doesn't acknowledge the so-called success I experience, I still see myself as a failure. I just work on what I must to make her happy."

Mike raised his eyebrows thoughtfully. "There are a lot of people around you that you could impress. Why your mother?"

Lisa paused, her expression becoming serious. "I've seen her suffer and struggle for the family after the divorce from my alcoholic dad." She fell silent for a moment, her face flushed with emotion. For about 60 seconds, she didn't speak.

"Lisa, are you okay? Should we continue?" Mike asked gently.

After a deep inhale and exhale, she replied, "Yes, we can continue. I've seen her struggle... I loathe my dad for that." She spoke slowly, still panting from the emotional weight of her words.

Seeing her distress, Mike stood up from his chair and offered her a glass of water. "Okay, Lisa, let's take a five-minute break."

She nodded gratefully and took a sip, quenching her thirst.

"Welcome back, Lisa," Mike said with a smirk as they resumed. "Now, I'd love for us to do something different. It's a deep breathing exercise. Please rise from your seat," he instructed.

"Stand straight, put your right hand on your stomach and your left palm at chest level. Breathe in for five seconds and breathe out for two seconds. Make sure you inhale through your nose, not your mouth. Let the air fill your belly; as you do, your right hand on your stomach should move while the left hand stays still," Mike instructed.

Lisa stood there, surprised, and asked, "What can this exercise do for me, Coach?"

"You've asked the right question. Breathing helps reduce stress and pain, especially from emotional experiences like the one you're facing. It can also improve focus, which is important for overcoming depression. I want us to do it together," he replied.

"Great, okay, let's try it together," Lisa said, eager to participate.

As they engaged in the breathing exercise, Mike guided her, "Lisa, don't think about any pain you're going through. Inhale for five seconds and exhale for two seconds, breathe through your nose. Good, let's try it again." He encouraged her with a calm demeanor.

"Feel free to take a sip of water. How do you feel after this short exercise?" he asked.

"I'm okay, better than before," she responded, a hint of relief in her voice. "And are you ready to continue?"

"Yes, I am!" she said, excitement bubbling up inside her.

Both of them sat adjacent to each other in a relaxed manner.

"Did your mind go back to any encounters? I'm talking about how your mother struggled to raise you after your dad left," he asked.

"Absolutely," she replied. "I remember there were frequent arguments between my parents. It felt like there was no peace in our lives or our home. I have a twin sister, Lily, who was always the apple of our mother's eye, while I was my father's favorite. It felt like there was divided parental love for us. Every time they fought, I got the smallest portion of food during lunch and dinner while my sister got the biggest chunk. My mom would call me unpleasant names because I resembled him so much.

After he left and divorced my mom, she struggled to care for my sister and me. It was as if she ensured I passed through the same pain she experienced. I always carried the same burden of pain while my sister enjoyed the best of everything. I felt left behind during my childhood, and it continued until I left home. I feel a surge of rage whenever I hear my dad's name because he left me at my mother's mercy. I believe if he had been around, I would have received more love from him."

"I see," Mike replied thoughtfully. "Did you ever discover why your mother hated your dad?"

"From their heated conversations during my childhood, I gathered that my dad was wealthy but didn't know how to manage money well and ended up going bankrupt. Instead of trying his best, he became an alcoholic, and that was the boiling point of their fights. They were always at each other's throats," Lisa explained.

"How did this affect you?" Mike asked gently.

"It made me feel very ugly inside. I wanted them to love each other and fight together through tough times. It was like everyone was on a blaming spree, pointing fingers at each other for the mistakes made. My dad was depressed a lot, and I started feeling the brunt of my mother's frustration when she felt she couldn't carry all the burdens alone. I was blamed for everything going wrong, which baffled me. Why was I to blame for all the chaos?"

Michael placed his fingers on his jawline, listening intently. "When did you start feeling this from your mother? How did it make you feel?"

"Home felt like a prison of confusion for me. I dreaded coming home from school or visiting the park because home was filled with noise and conflict. I lost my admiration for the idea of a perfect home," Lisa admitted, her voice heavy with emotion.

"During that encounter, I wished I could shout in rage to release all the troubles I've encountered in my life," Lisa confessed, her voice trembling with emotion.

"Can you shout now?" Mike asked. "If you're worried about disturbing anyone in this building, don't be. This place is soundproof, so no one will hear you."

Lisa looked perplexed at Michael's suggestion, placing her index finger against her cheek. "I can shout, Coach! But I don't feel like doing that right now."

"Anytime you feel the urge to shout and release the pent-up rage inside you, we'll try it," he reassured her.

Lisa nodded in affirmation, considering the idea.

"Well, such an experience," Mike continued. "When you were going through this, did it ever cross your mind to reach out to family members for help?"

"I tried to find a few relatives," she replied. "To my surprise, none of them wanted to help my family. They felt my parents were reserved and sensitive and thought they would figure it out themselves. Since no one reported the issues to other family members—especially the trusted ones—they believed it was the McShan family's problem to solve, which was impossible. I think my mom has some misconceptions about me; she doesn't really believe me."

"When did you start trying to impress her?" Mike asked gently.

"I realized that the only way to find some happiness was to join them," Lisa explained. "There's a popular quote from my friend Lucy: 'If you can't beat them, join them.' I had to wipe away all the negative thoughts I had towards her and replace them with good ones. Even amidst all the noise in the house, I still love her. I wanted to impress her, to make her happy so I could feel cheerful and find some peace. But that led me to receive certain information that compounded my hatred towards my dad."

"Did anything change when you did that? Did trying to impress her lead her to love you like your sister?" Mike probed.

Lisa sat quietly for a moment, contemplating. "Hmm, nothing changed. From that encounter, despite my efforts to impress her, there was no positive change. She always compared me to others and set high challenges for me. She made it clear that nothing I did was successful while others were moving ahead. I often felt like I was stuck at level one or at the bottom. She would say things like, 'You're just a working person, not successful.'"

"From the age of ten to thirty-two, I've tried to impress her to be considered a good daughter like my twin sister, but nothing has changed. This has become my life—impressing people all the time."

"I see where the problem lies," Mike said thoughtfully. "Did you gain anything from it?"

"No," Lisa shook her head. "Everyone I tried to impress always betrayed me. They never appreciated what I did for them."

"Will you continue with this act?" he asked.

"No, it's not helping me at all. I'm always hurt. I try to stop but can't," she admitted, her voice heavy with resignation.

"Let's do this. I want you to tell me what you see," Mike said as he stood up and brought a beaker of water and a color pigment to the table. "Lisa, what do you see on this table? What did I just bring here?"

"Come on, Coach, it's a beaker of water and a color pigment," she responded, raising an eyebrow in awe.

"The beaker filled with water is so clear that we can see what's inside," Lisa began. "It represents a life filled with joy, focus, and happiness. The pigment, on the other hand, is filled with chemicals that come together to form a dye. We all know that chemicals, when used too often, can harm us. The dye is not as clear as the water; it symbolizes a life of unclear objectives, lack of focus, and being a people pleaser."

"When I pour the dye into the water, what will happen?" Michael asked.

"It will turn a red color because the dye is red," Lisa replied.

"You're right. Now, if I put a red eraser in there, would you see it?" he continued.

"No, because they're the same color," she answered.

"What do you illustrate from this regarding your life?" he probed further.

"Though these are examples, I see that when I pour the dye filled with my unfocused and people-pleasing lifestyle into the clear water, which represents a focused and happy person, it changes color. The ink corrupts the whole body of a clear, focused, and happier person into a negative one."

"With your case, what can you do to remain happier?" Michael encouraged her.

"I need to clear my life to become more focused and stop the need to impress others," Lisa said firmly. "I've allowed a confused, unfocused person to change me into someone negative. I have to put a stop to that mindset and behavior."

"Oh, yes, that's a good suggestion," Michael acknowledged, nodding.

He handed her a black hardcover notebook with crème-lined paper. "Here, Lisa. Use this to record all the pain and tell me what you think. Write about all your encounters with your parents. Write everything you've experienced, your feelings, and your thoughts. Reflect on whether it was good to bring you to this point in the first place."

"Thank you, I will work on it," she replied, feeling a sense of purpose.

"It looks like our session is up. See you in a week, same time?" he asked.

"Absolutely, same time," she agreed, feeling lighter as she left the room, ready to embark on her journey of self-discovery and healing.

# Impress Others

"After my first session with you a week ago, you know you gave me a task to do on my own," Lisa began, her voice a mix of excitement and apprehension.

"Absolutely! How can I forget? Were you able to work on it?" Michael asked, leaning forward, interested.

"Yes, I did! At first, I thought the notebook was something for teens. Holding it reminded me of my younger days when my friends and I used to write in notebooks or diaries about our thoughts and feelings. It was such a good outlet for us back then, but I thought we'd outgrown it," she said, her face lighting up with nostalgia.

"I'm glad the notebook brought back those childhood memories! It's a great way to get all your worries out on paper. That's fantastic! What did you write about?" he encouraged her.

"A lot happened. I cried after reading what I had written in the book. Unleashing more memories onto the page made me realize I've been ruled by this need to impress others my whole life," Lisa confessed.

"Really? Can you share what happened? The more you speak about it, the more you free your thoughts," Michael urged gently.

"Why not? This time, I won't be panting," she said, a newfound strength evident in her voice. "It's like freeing my being into this notebook has given me the courage to push further. One memory stood out during my family's pressure, just like we discussed last week.

"One cloudy Monday during recess at school, I saw my friend Rachel talking to two guys at the entrance of the main hall. I walked over with a smile, eager to join them. Since their backs were turned, Rachel was the only one who saw me approaching."

Michael listened attentively, his right index finger resting on his jawline, absorbing her words.

"Then, I noticed Rachel roll her eyes at me, which struck me as strange because I didn't want to believe a friend would do something like that. I took about five steps closer, but suddenly Rachel whispered something to one of the guys. They both turned to look at me, smirking and laughing. One guy said, 'An alcoholic dad? Shame on you!'

"In that moment, I felt a cold wave wash over me. I was confused, thinking, 'Who spilled the beans to these guys?' I felt so exposed when Rachel laughed with them and mocked me right there in front of everyone. The hallway was crowded, and they called me names as if it was some kind of joke."

Lisa paused, the hurt from that memory evident in her eyes.

"At that moment, I felt terrible about myself. The noise, my dad's divorce from the family, and his behavior as an alcoholic were all draining me. I remembered confiding in Rachel about my family's struggles, hoping for some companionship in the midst of my dismay. But in that moment, all I could feel was regret for trusting her. I thought sharing my truth would bring peace, but instead, I felt more alone than ever."

"What happened next?" Michael asked, leaning in with interest.

"I didn't know what was going on. The only person who knew the truth was the same one mocking me in front of others, calling me names. Tears began to stream down my cheeks as one of them mimicked, 'Crying Lisa!'"

Lisa's voice cracked slightly, and she took a deep breath. "My heart was racing, and I couldn't control the chaos in my mind. I thought I was getting comfort from Rachel, but instead, I cried bitterly and ran to the janitor's closet."

"The only thought that kept repeating in my mind was 'I was betrayed.'" Both Lisa and Michael said this in unison, and Lisa smiled faintly.

"I felt utterly betrayed. No one knew my family's secrets, which Rachel had now exposed. She was the only person I confided in because home was not a safe place for me. I wanted to be close to the 'cool kids' and feel happier. I just wanted to fit in. Because of that, I made the final decision to impress others, especially my friends.

"Family was important to me. I thought it would be better to fit in with my mother than with anyone else, whether I liked it or not. Blood ties are stronger, and the betrayal of a family member feels worse than that from a friend. Before I made that final decision that ended up ruling my life, I met Lucy in the janitor's closet.

"She found me sitting on the floor, my head resting on my knees, wailing. Suddenly, I felt a tap on my shoulder. I lifted my face, tears streaming down my cheeks and smudging my blouse. I was shaken when I saw it was Lucy. At that time, she wasn't really a friend—just a classmate."

"Why are you crying?" she asked, genuinely curious.

I didn't want to respond because I didn't want to dive deeper into my sadness.

"She kept asking until I finally replied, 'I was just betrayed a few minutes ago.' She tried to comfort me, but I wasn't ready to listen; I had already convinced myself that things were hopeless."

"I see. What did you feel when you read this in your notebook?" Michael inquired, wanting to dig deeper.

"I was furious with myself for letting myself fall into that mess. I felt pity for my younger self, wondering why I made that decision at such a young age. I allowed others' happiness to jeopardize my own life and well-being."

"Okay, do you want to blame others or yourself for this, Lisa?" he asked gently.

"Not at all, coach. Blaming others would lead me into another nightmare, and I don't want to become a negative person."

Michael nodded, a smile on his face. "Let's do this: Imagine you could travel back in time to your teenage years with your mother. What advice would you give the younger Lisa who was facing these challenges?"

"If I could, I would tell myself so many things," Lisa began, her eyes sparkling with determination. "First, I would upgrade my mindset and not focus on the noise around me. I would draw closer to things that bring me peace, like journaling, engaging in hobbies such as reading and singing, and truly enjoying the natural beauty of parks. Back then, I would visit Green Park, but I didn't appreciate how that peaceful environment could contribute to my personal growth.

"I would also reach out to an adult for guidance, someone who could nurture my mindset, even if others saw my family as sensitive. Lastly, I wouldn't allow the opinions or actions of people to dictate my focus or force me to please them just to fit in. I would do everything necessary to cultivate a sense of peace and total happiness in my life."

"That's great! What are you going to do more to be yourself now?" Michael asked, leaning forward with interest.

"I will stop every boundary that prevents me from finding peace," Lisa replied, her voice steady. "Peace in a sense that I won't let anyone compare me to others, instill doubt in me, or blame me. I've realized that I'm still young and fragile in this regard. This is my commitment: to silence the noise that makes me doubt myself."

"I'm also going to create a fundamental rule to guide my life: you can't impress everyone in this world. As humans, we have unlimited needs, so you can never please everyone. Since I know the difference between good and evil, I will focus on doing the right thing and pleasing myself instead."

"Awesome!" he responded, his face lighting up with enthusiasm. "Those are nice strategies. I want you to create a set of rules to follow daily based on what you just said. Write them down in your notebook or on a sticky note in a visible place at home, on your PC, or on your mobile phone. Take it slow; don't rush yourself if you can't follow it every day. Mistakes are part of the journey—don't let them stop you."

"I'd like you to track your daily activities related to your mindset. For example, if someone acknowledges how wonderful you are and you start to doubt yourself, write that down. Or if you realize you are special and successful, record that too. You can review your progress weekly, bi-weekly, or monthly to see how well you're believing in yourself and distancing yourself from people-pleasing. This will help you track your mindset and behaviors, and hopefully turn them into routines that become part of who you are."

"Also, I don't want you to neglect journaling, walking in the park, or any other self-improvement habits just because you're focused on replacing people-pleasing. Value these activities and understand their importance in your life."

Lisa smiled, her cheeks brightening at his encouragement. "With my palms together, I appreciate this advice. Thank you so much!"

"Keep going, Lisa. Remember, this is your journey to becoming the best version of yourself," Michael said, his eyes filled with encouragement. "I'm excited to see how you grow."

# Don't focus too much on the words you hear

Lisa raised her eyebrows, letting out a thoughtful sigh. She looked eager to voice something to Michael. "Coach, I've been wondering about this and would like to ask you. Why do you want to help women with their self-discovery, self-love, and mindset? You're a man; you could be doing this for men instead."

Michael smiled and waved his fingers as if inviting her to explore the topic. "Lisa, I was actually expecting you to ask me that question at the beginning of our first session, so I'm glad you did. I've had this question come up countless times."

Lisa sat up attentively, eager to hear his response.

"Back in my teens, my mother was in an abusive relationship with my dad, where she faced emotional abuse and bullying. It deeply affected her self-esteem; she believed that her worth was contingent on others' approval. If people accepted her, she felt okay, but if not, she felt worthless. After the divorce, those negative behaviors persisted and only intensified, causing her anxiety. As I grew up, I made it my mission to help her and others like her. So, I decided to become a life coach."

He paused for a moment, letting the weight of his words settle in. "Through guidance, mentoring, and prayers, I helped her transform. She's a new person now, deeply rooted in personal development. Today, she helps other women who once faced similar challenges, empowering them to develop self-confidence and self-love, and guiding them away from abusive relationships."

"That's incredible," Lisa replied, feeling inspired. "It's clear your mom is dear to you."

"Yes, you're right," Michael continued. "Seeing her struggle through that abusive relationship made me realize how crucial it is to support others in their journeys. I focus on helping women, but I don't neglect men either. I believe in guiding both, which is why I'm here for you."

"I can see that passion in you," Lisa said, her admiration growing. "It's a privilege to help others succeed in life and develop personally. I'm really excited about embarking on my own self-discovery journey."

"Absolutely, Lisa! I'm thrilled to see you embrace this path. Your journey to self-discovery and personal growth is important, and I'm here to support you every step of the way," Michael encouraged with a warm smile.

"I see parallels in your story and mine," Lisa reflected. "Although our experiences are different, the lessons and values we learn resonate deeply. If your mom could transform her life, that encourages me to work harder on myself too."

With a smile, Michael replied, "I'm glad you're ready to grow. Let's continue with your session. Has it ever crossed your mind that you might miss your dad?"

"Yes, I do a lot," Lisa admitted. "I wish I could do something to get closer to him again."

"And have you tried to contact or visit him?" Michael inquired gently.

"Yes, those thoughts have crossed my mind before," she said, hesitating. "But anything I do feels like it would hurt my mom. It seems like my dad has never been the best father to me, and I feel ungrateful for everything my mom sacrificed for my sister and me. She emphasizes that my dad's love is not something I should focus on. She tries her best to help me forget him."

"It sounds like you have the desire to communicate with your father, but your concern for your mother holds you back," Michael observed.

Lisa nodded, acknowledging the truth in his words.

"I hope you know you are entitled to the choices you make," Michael continued.

"Absolutely, I know that," Lisa replied. "Because the choices I make can lead to either business profits or losses, just like in my personal life."

"You own the choices you make in life, too," Michael emphasized. "Every decision leads to a responsibility. You must take responsibility and never let anyone choose for you. Think about it: even being here in this coaching session is a choice. You have the right to accept the tools, tips, and advice I give. It's all up to you."

Lisa listened intently. "I understand that if I choose not to visit or search for my dad, it's my decision, not my mother's. If he's not close and I don't feel okay when I think about him, I need to follow my heart and intuition."

Michael nodded, encouraging her. "Now, let's do this: Imagine you are your father, Mr. McShan. Think about all his experiences. If he didn't know where you were, especially knowing how successful you've become, what would you do?"

Lisa sat quietly for a minute, contemplating the question. Finally, she spoke softly, "I would be very sad, hurt, and regret not looking for my children after I divorced their mother. I would want to search for my children. Seeing Lisa as a successful woman, I would feel compelled to reach out because I'd believe she's hurt, which is why she hasn't contacted me. I would ask for forgiveness."

Michael smiled, recognizing the depth of her reflection. "That's a powerful realization, Lisa. Understanding how you might feel in your father's shoes can help you navigate your own feelings about him."

Michael looked at Lisa with sincerity. "This is what I'll tell you: go and search for your father. Inquire about what really happened, forgive him, and love him as you always wanted him to be. Though it can be hard, I want you to think about it, let go of all the grudges inside you, and bring peace to your heart. When you're ready, encourage your twin sister to do the same and work on rebuilding your bond with your father. I believe he is eager for your forgiveness and to be embraced by you again. They say blood is thicker than water, so follow your heart."

Lisa listened intently, absorbing his words. "With the scenarios I gave you, you could have responded in many ways, but you revealed this particular answer. I believe something inside you is communicating, paving the way for peace among yourselves. Please, just try it. Encourage your heart to be at peace with him."

"I will, coach," Lisa replied, a hint of resolve in her voice. "It seems like you're tapping into something emotional and spiritual here."

"I am," Michael admitted, nodding. "Everything around us consists of spirit, mind, and body. If your spirit and your dad's spirit are communicating about forgiveness, I think you should try to listen. Let's meet in two weeks' time."

"Thank you," Lisa said with gratitude. "I see today's session as one of the most emotional and heartfelt experiences I've had. All the tools and tips you've given me will definitely help me push my personal development to the next level."

Michael smiled, feeling a sense of accomplishment for the progress they had made together. "I look forward to hearing about your journey in our next session, Lisa. Remember, it's all about taking those small steps toward healing and growth."

# Rethink about life

They stood in pin-drop silence, eagerly watching as Lisa spoke. She had invited the business development team back to her office after the incident with the Events and Associates tender, and everyone was curious about what she would say next.

"I guess you're doing great," Lisa said, looking around the room.

"Yes, we are," they collectively responded, though their faces betrayed a hint of anxiety.

"Your faces look like your hearts are about to jump out of your chests," Lisa noted, smiling. "Steven, is that true?"

"We're a bit nervous about what will happen after the incident and the punishment attached to it. Sorry if our faces tell it all," Steven admitted.

Lisa smiled reassuringly. "Never mind. I'm not going to punish you for a mistake. I want to ask you, what lessons have you learned from your experience with the concert chairs tender?"

Evana spoke up. "We should always be careful with any documents we submit, whether to you or outside parties. We must be vigilant and double-check everything before submission."

"Okay, that's nice, Evana. I'm glad you've learned something," Lisa replied, encouragingly. "Upon serious consideration of any punishment for your negligence regarding that tender, I've decided to cancel the 15% salary reduction I proposed the other day. You shouldn't be blamed for anything related to that. Things happen for a reason, and we learn from our mistakes. We shouldn't dwell on them or let them leave a regrettable mark on our lives. Life must go on."

A wave of relief washed over the team, and they smiled brightly as Lisa spoke.

"Let's make Lisa Initiatives one of the best companies in the area and region. My advice to you is to embrace every challenge you face, avoid complaining or blaming anyone, and instead, work to overcome any problems."

As Lisa finished her speech, Evans spoke up. "Thank you, ma'am. We appreciate this, and your advice will be a daily reminder for us in both life and at this company. Thank you once again!"

Lisa nodded, beaming with pride. "Now, you can return to your respective work posts."

As the team left her office, Lucy met them in the hallway. She gave a curious glance at the team as they walked out and then turned back to Lisa, who sat in her chair with a sweet countenance.

"Did I miss something?" Lucy asked.

Lisa leaned back in her chair, gently swinging it from side to side. "No, my friend. This time, something has changed for the better. I lifted the 15% salary reduction and gave them some advice."

"This is amazing, Lisa! Really good news for your team. Now I understand why their faces look so bright—and yours too!

You're radiating positive energy today. It's like a miracle has happened. I guess your sessions with the coach are helping, right?" Lucy inquired.

"You're right. I feel kind of relieved after the first stage with Michael. I'm seeing positive changes in myself. I know I'm just getting started, and I'm eager to initiate my self-discovery using his techniques."

"I told you so! I'm 100% glad that you gave it a try and are making amends for your past mistakes. I'm rooting for you. Keep going!" Lucy encouraged, her eyes sparkling with enthusiasm.

Lisa smiled, feeling a sense of hope and determination. "Thanks, Lucy. Your support means a lot."

# Believe in yourself.

After two weeks of personal care and heeding the advice of her coach, Lisa was ready for another session with Michael. She was determined to work on the tools and strategies he had provided to improve her life. As she waited for him to arrive, her cheerful demeanor reflected the progress she had made.

When Michael walked in, he immediately noticed the spark of happiness on her face. "Your face is glowing with excitement!" he exclaimed.

"I'm so happy! Can you guess what really happened?" Lisa quizzed, her eyes shining with enthusiasm.

"Unless you tell me, I won't know," he replied with a warm smile.

"I can finally bond with my dad! I've forgiven him, and he's forgiven me for not reaching out sooner. I was surprised at how eager he was to clear the air about what happened years ago. It really made me realize that our world consists of body, mind, and spirit, just like you advised a few weeks ago. It felt like everything was connected, and we were both searching for each other without knowing how," Lisa explained, her voice filled with joy.

"I also convinced my sister to bond with him, and it was easier than I expected! She was eager to talk to him and had so many questions. It felt like the universe was aligning for us, and God was orchestrating our reunion."

"Wow, that's incredible news! How did you manage to get his contact?" Michael asked, genuinely interested.

"I reached out to an uncle of mine, who is also my dad's brother, for his contact information. He even accompanied me to my dad's house. The atmosphere was filled with connection and tears of joy. Afterward, I encouraged my sister to meet him too," Lisa recounted, a broad smile spreading across her face.

Michael nodded, impressed. "That sounds like a powerful experience. What was your mum's reaction to all of this?"

Lisa's expression softened slightly as she thought about her mother. "At first, she was surprised. I think it caught her off guard. But once I explained everything, she was supportive. I know she's worried about how it might affect us, but I assured her that it's about healing and moving forward as a family. I want to show her that we can all have our own paths while still valuing what she's done for us."

"It's great that you're considering her feelings, too. This is a significant step for all of you. How do you feel about it all?" Michael asked, leaning in closer.

"I feel liberated and hopeful! I never realized how much holding onto that grudge weighed me down. Now that I've let it go, I feel like I can breathe again. It's like a weight has been lifted off my shoulders," Lisa replied, her smile growing wider.

"I'm so proud of you, Lisa. This is a testament to your growth and willingness to embrace change. Keep this momentum going as you continue your journey of self-discovery," Michael encouraged, beaming with pride.

"Thank you, coach! Your guidance has made all the difference. I'm excited for what's next," Lisa said, her enthusiasm infectious as they prepared to dive deeper into her personal development.

"You can't imagine the reaction on my mother's face when my younger sister decided to visit our dad," Lisa said with a chuckle. "It was like going to a football match knowing you're going to lose. It really hurt her when she heard that Lily was going to see him; it felt like her labor had been in vain. I think she needs to heal too."

Lisa smiled as she spoke, the weight of the situation lifting off her shoulders. "But I'm so glad I reached out. I feel at peace now. It's like the need to impress my mother and others has faded away. I don't care what she says about my success or failure anymore. It's my life, and I have the choice to be happier and focus on where I want to be. The most important thing is that I have peace of mind in my heart and mind."

Michael nodded, a proud smile on his face. "I'm excited for you! It's great to see how this peace has changed not only your outlook but even the way you talk. Your energy is so bright and positive now. Remember to love both of your parents equally. Just because you've seen your dad doesn't mean you should stop caring for your mom. Focus less on impressing her or anyone else."

"Noted, coach," Lisa acknowledged, feeling empowered as she continued the conversation. "I was a little down when the mindset tracking didn't go as planned, but then I remembered my story from childhood to adulthood has taught me that life is never perfect. When life gives you lemons..."

"Make lemonade!" they both chimed in, laughing.

"Exactly! You told me that even if the tracking doesn't go as planned, I shouldn't give up. It's about embracing my imperfections. I don't care about the bad reviews from customers anymore; I see them as motivation to improve my work."

"Great to hear! So, do you still want people to praise you before you see yourself as successful?" Michael asked.

"Not all, coach. That was my previous self. Now I know what I possess and I believe in myself. Even when things don't go well in my business or life, I don't waste time blaming others. The mindset tracking journal has truly saved my life."

"Wonderful to hear, Lisa! It sounds like you've really embraced the tools."

"Since I understand that what the mind thinks shapes my reality, I created another journal to track the things I do—fun activities, impactful moments, adventures, and even mistakes. I record them daily, and at the end of the week, I review them to see my strengths, interests, and what I shouldn't repeat. It's really helped me believe in my potential. I don't wait for others to tell me, 'Lisa, you are successful, smart, intelligent, or beautiful.' I already know those things and work towards them. Even if someone tells me something I don't know, I take it as a chance to be self-aware and discover the truth for myself."

"That's an amazing shift in mindset!" Michael praised. "I'm thrilled to see how far you've come."

"I've also started affirming positive words and being kinder to myself. I write these affirmations in a notebook to train my mind to recognize me as successful Lisa. I've noticed significant improvements. I wouldn't say I'm fully there yet, but I've transformed into a better version of myself."

"This is incredible transformation!" Michael responded joyfully, applauding for Lisa. "Your journey is inspiring, and I'm so proud of you for putting in the work. Keep it up, and remember, growth is a continuous process. You're on the right path!"

Lisa beamed with gratitude, feeling empowered and ready for whatever came next in her journey of self-discovery.

# Definition of success

A phone beeped, breaking the moment of reflection.

"Lisa, it seems your phone is ringing," Michael urged, glancing at her with a knowing look.

"Never mind, coach," Lisa replied, brushing it off.

"I think it might be something important. Who knows?" he said, his tone suggesting he believed she should check.

Lisa glanced at the screen, seeing "Davis Michaels" flashing.

"It's Davis!" she exclaimed, picking up the call and initiating the conversation. "It's been a while, Davis."

"Hi, Lisa," he replied. "I personally wanted to call to inform you about the new contract. We decided to add more to the 45 corporate clients we discussed almost a month ago after the 100 million tender announcement at my office. You will be delivering corporate chairs and other furniture to 200 companies on our database for the next five years, which is subject to renewal. I've sent the contract via email; kindly read, sign, and get back to us."

With a joyful tone, Lisa responded, "That is awesome! I will get back to you in a week with the signed copy of the contract."

"You can take as long as you need to understand it well, which will benefit both your company and ours. Can't wait to do business with you," Davis said, his excitement evident.

They exchanged closing remarks and ended the call.

Lisa turned to Michael, her eyes sparkling. "I see the heavens are working for my good. After finding peace of mind and learning to love who I am now, things are changing. Guess what? The sole reason that led me to you for guidance is this company!"

"I guess you know Events and Associates?" she continued, her voice filled with enthusiasm.

"Totally! Why not? They are one of the top event organizers in this country and have been in the market for over 20 years," Michael affirmed.

"Great! I was initially eager to win their 100 million tender contract, which didn't come through. That made me angry and led me to question why they didn't award it to me. Meanwhile, on the same day, they offered me another opportunity, but I didn't appreciate that because I was too focused on impressing my mom and others to gain their acceptance."

Michael nodded, understanding the struggle she faced. "It's natural to seek validation, but it's wonderful to see how you've shifted your perspective. Now you're realizing your own worth and the opportunities that come your way."

"Exactly! I've learned that sometimes the doors we think are closing are actually leading us to better opportunities," Lisa said, feeling the weight of her previous frustrations lift.

"Keep that mindset, Lisa. Embrace the journey, and continue building on this newfound confidence. You're doing amazing things!" Michael encouraged, proud of her progress.

"Thank you, coach. I'm ready to tackle this new contract and make it a success!" Lisa declared, filled with determination and excitement for the future.

"I am grateful for Lucy for appearing in my office that day. As a result of that encounter, I placed my anger on my staff, and even Lucy had her share of it. But this did not discourage her. She knew who I was and managed to encourage me to seek help to remodel my mindset and pursue self-discovery. Now, I have gained a lot for my personal development, and I'm also thrilled about this new contract. I can't believe it! Previously, Events and Associates proposed 45 clients, and now it's 200 companies for delivery. I truly understand now that my transformation was destined to happen."

"Great turnaround story!" Michael responded, beaming with pride.

"Imagine if they had called to give you just the 45 clients. Would you be happy?" he asked curiously.

"I would be, but I know there are reasons why things happen. With those 45 clients, if they are satisfied, they will become evangelists for my business. Even if it's just one person, I strongly believe in customer service and quality. One person can be an advocate for my business. After all, one person is better than zero clients. It's about making small improvements in everything."

"Do you mean that as long as there are small steps, that's all that matters?" Michael inquired.

"Absolutely. It's all about appreciating what I have, rather than waiting for a big difference before I appreciate it. If I can appreciate the small wins when they come, I can appreciate the big ones when they arrive," Lisa explained with conviction.

"Thank you, coach, for taking the time to nurture my thoughts, mindset, and for helping me learn to love myself too. I really appreciate it," Lisa said gratefully.

"You're very welcome. It is my duty as your coach to help you see the things about yourself that you might not notice. I'm glad my work to assist you is progressing, but it's not fully done. I will be following up to see how you improve," Michael replied, his tone encouraging.

"Before you leave to fulfill your greatness with the things you've discovered here, what are you going to do to rule your life?" he asked, his eyes focused on her.

"I appreciate that question. I will focus on myself and not worry about what others think. I don't need to impress anyone to be authentic; I need to impress myself and embrace the real me. Most importantly, I want to use the little I've gained here to help my mother too. With the knowledge I've gained, I see that she's still in pain, which needs healing. My sister and I will join forces to show her the way," Lisa affirmed, her voice filled with determination.

Michael smiled in affirmation. "What a powerful closing remark! Go and make yourself happier and change the world with self-love."

With that, Lisa felt a renewed sense of purpose. She was ready to embrace her journey, not just for herself, but also for her family.

63

# Conclusion

What's your takeaway from Lisa's story?

Self-love is essential in our daily lives and helps us achieve our dreams. Never underestimate its power—the parts of yourself that you may ignore or dislike could hold the key to your greatness. Keep moving forward, and let kindness and gratitude guide you, both toward yourself and others.

# Self-love Code

Using the lessons inside this book. Develop your ten codes to self-love which you will be using to guide your life.

# Next in the series

# Gratitude Notes

**Do you believe in gratitude?**

How often do you show thankfulness to yourself and others? Do you often believe that things must move on smoothly with you before you show appreciation?

This is a story of gratitude intertwined with pain and unforgiveness through a story told by a young gentleman who experienced trauma in childhood. He encountered the ups and downs as he journeyed through life.

The mistakes he experienced led him to find the truth about his identity and life.

Discover more about gratitude, peace, happiness and better living.

**Recommended Books and Journals from My Library**

If you want to upgrade your life and work on your dreams, I recommend the following books from my coffers.

**'Win You'**

Self-awareness matters when you want to know more about yourself. Build life by knowing what you possess with 'Win You.'

**'Lift it High'**

It is filled with messages and steps that can motivate you to do good for your life. It spreads across all areas that can help you to turn your dreams into realities, like thought, mind power, belief in yourself, gratitude, influence and many more.

**The Search Workbook**

Finding gratitude can never be left out when it comes to purpose. Your soul search exercise is important. It contains questions that can guide your life to the greatest extent and fill it with a journey.

Emotional Release Journal

It is filled with questions where you can release all the pain, fears and negative emotions that dull your shine.

Goal Setter and Implementer

Our goals are important when it comes to our search for self-love. We need to set those goals too. Goal Setter and Implementer Journal will set, manage and implement your track your goals.

# Everything about Brigitte

# SPREAD THE WORD!

**Do this to help spread the message and help others.**

Here are some activities you can do to help them out.

> Write a review on any other marketplace where you bought this book. This will help other readers to know how valuable this book is and how it can help them out by providing an honest review.

> Send an email to me on how this book is helping you and other loved ones. This email message can serve as a motivation and inspiration to me to write more books that solve your problems in life. Send it via brigitte@brigitteaagyapongwrites.com

> Share a page where you read a favorite quote or message inside this book on social media. Also, you can share an image of yourself reading this book. Tag me on Instagram via @brigitteauthor or on Facebook @inspired by Brigitte.

> Practice every bit of the lesson inside this book.

> Live an exemplary life for others.

> Recommend to 50 people what this book is helping you with and it contains. You might an avenue of growth in other people life.

**BRIGITTE ADOFO AGYAPONG, Life Coach**

Do you wish to discover your true potential?

Would you like to use your abilities to work for your dreams and turn them into success?

Or do you want to set all goals to assist you in turning your dream projects into reality?

Would you like to hire a life coach to reach your personal goals faster?

Then Visit:

https://www.brigittaagyapongwrites.com

# Connect with me

Email: contactus@brigitteaagyapongwrites.com

Website: www.brigitteaagyapongwrites.com[1]

Facebook @inspired by Brigitte.

Instagram @brigitteauthor

TikTok @brigittewrites_motivates

YouTube
https://www.youtube.com/@Elevatedmindset.Brigitte

Goodreads https://www.goodreads.com/brigitteauthor

Bookbub: www.bookbub/author/Brigitteagyapong/[2]

---

1. http://www.brigitteaagyapongwrites.com

2. http://www.bookbub/author/Brigitteagyapong/

**Tune in to Elevate with Brigitte Podcast Show**

One of the Initiatives Brigitte uses to spread her message of hope, greatness, possibilities and fulfilment is through her life-changing podcast, Elevate with Brigitte Podcast Show.

On her podcast show, she shares messages that will help upgrade your life and push you to greatness. She believes there all a whole lot of things you can do with your potential: achieve your dreams, help others achieve theirs, become an influence in other people's lives and many actions that we can do to turn our dreams around and grow.

With Elevate with Brigitte, you would have access to enjoy development in areas like purpose, mindset, emotions, love, achieving your dreams, supporting others and many more.

Guess what? Every Wednesday, a new episode goes live. You can tune it on Spotify, Google Podcast, , Audible, Radio Public, Pandora, Player fm, Pocket Cast, TuneIn, Pod Vine, and my website www.brigitteaagyapongwrites.com/podcast/

## About the Book

She is successful. Lisa McShan is a founder and CEO of her firm and wish she would win the 100 million worth value of contract. She thought she was an inch of winning it. Her expectation are high even when other opportunities comes way, she is no allowing them to come her mind.

Her mind so fixed on the high goal of that worth of contract.

This leads her to something else. Her desire and energy were on it.

Through one high expectation leads her to break her past and give in peace to herself.

Discover Lisa's journey to self-love, belongness and kindness as she experiences the journey along in this book.

## About the Author

Brigitte Adofo Agyapong is an author, life coach, podcast host, motivator, and a personal development enthusiast. She has author over 13 books and counting, and the Podcast Host, of Elevate with Brigitte, a personal development show on assisting listeners to harness themselves and work on their dreams to bring the maximum output to them and the society.

She believes that our dreams cannot be accomplished when we don't believe in ourselves, and the qualities we possess, and in addition to that love ourselves no matter the obstruction we might faces.